Today I Cook!

A Man's Guide to the kitchen!

Felix Weber

Schiffer Publishing Ltd®

4880 Lower Valley Road, Atglen, Pennsylvania 19310

FOREword

Why shouldn't a man be able to cook? After all, it makes him independent, and unbelievably sexy. It's just a matter of overcoming his inner beast. Once this is done, the cooking can begin.

When thinking about preparing food, a man can get easily distracted when he starts facing the challenges of cooking. He thinks:

"Buy the ingredients, measure them, mix them, finished—that is so simple! I'll invite Susie to dinner on Sunday, and my cooking skills will surely make an impression.

Just remember: $\dfrac{(x + 5)\,2 - y^2}{x^2\,(y - 3^x)}$ = time needed for a juicy roast! Rare roast beef—heavens, that will take a long time! I really wanted to watch the game, at least for a little bit.

Cooking, Susie, the game, (gasp), wash dishes, clean up the kitchen...And Sunday is all over.

Maybe I can plan it all a little better, especially if I want to dish out the whole menu: soup or appetizer, main dish, and maybe dessert. Then I'll just have to pass on the game today. One just can't have everything."

That approach makes it all seem overwhelming. So, here is the secret weapon for irresistible recipes, helpful tips and tricks, and amazing knowledge that will take you from having nothing to show in the kitchen to showing off. Only then will things go well with Susie, too.

CONtents

1. Small, but Nice— Always Go Over Well

2. Simple Menus— They Always Work

3. A Little More Effort— Will Impress Susie

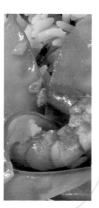

4. The Whole Enchilada

COOKING school

Before a man really cuts loose,
he should consider a few basic things:

1. Clear all work surfaces! Your wallet, cell phone, car keys, pocket knife, flashlights, or screws should not be strewn about on your work surface. Now there should be room for a nice big cutting board.

2. Washing your hands goes without saying. To be cautious, put on an apron. If you have hair like a young Jon Bon Jovi, use a chef's hat or a hair band. Nothing is more unappealing than a bowl of soup with hair in it!

3. ALWAYS read through the complete recipe first, before you start cooking.

4. You will need several bowls of varying sizes. Metal or tempered glass are the best materials for your bowls. Plastic bowls melt pretty quickly on, or even near, a hot burner.

5. The best cookware are pots with a firm straight bottom. Pots and pans with dents and dings on the bottom eat up energy and are not efficient. Also, check that there is no damage to the coating on your pans. To start, it's best to leave the pressure cooker in the cupboard.

6. ATTENTION: The general rule is to not place food covered in aluminum foil in the microwave, as the metal blocks the microwaves and prevents the food from cooking. But sometimes wrapping the ends of

poultry bones will keep the meat from overcooking. But be sure to read the manual before cooking with metal in your microwave.

7. Every good cook has a set of knives with a good variety, from small paring knives to potato peelers to big meat and vegetable knives.

8. Put all the ingredients you plan to cook with within reach before you start!

Quantities Needed for One Person

This can naturally be used to calculate for more people. Thus you should keep in mind who is coming to eat. Children and old people eat a lot less then, for example, a teenager. So these values are just guidelines.		
Meat for roasting or cutlets, w/ bones	$\geq^1/_2$ lb	250 g
Meat for roasting or cutlets, w/o bones	$>^1/_3$ lb	200 g
Beef steak or fish fillet	$>^1/_3$ lb	200 g
Breaded cutlets	$>^1/_3$ lb	180 g
Vegetables as a side dish	$\sim^1/_3$ lb	150–200 g
Potatoes as a side dish	$1^1/_2$ medium potatoes	200 g
Rice as side dish	$^1/_8$ - $^1/_4$ cup	30–40 g
Noodles as side dish	$3^1/_2$ - $5^1/_4$ oz	100–150 g
Rice as a main course	$^1/_4$ - $^1/_3$ cup	50–60 g
Noodles as a main course	7 - $8^3/_4$ oz	200–250 g
Soup as appetizer	1 cup	(1/4 l)
Soup as main course	2 cups	(1/2 l)
Sauce or gravy	$^1/_2$ cup	$^1/_8$ l

Culinary First Aid:

One knife point?
Will that be enough?

Salt in the Soup

Sometimes "the salt in the soup" is too much. So, what can you do about it? In clear soups one can usually help by adding water. In thicker soups, for example, cream, milk, or egg may help. Simply add it to the soup and season carefully.

Noodles are too soft

If the noodles have become almost too soft, drain quickly and rinse in cold water so they do not continue to overcook.

Burned (in the pot)

If the dish isn't too viscous, immediately (every second matters!) pour the contents into a fresh pot. Never help it along with a spoon in the same pot. Whatever remains stuck, leave it stuck. For solid foods, carefully remove the contents from the scorched pot and put them into a fresh pot. Leave large scorched pieces in the pot. If you scrape out pieces of the scorched food, everything can be spoiled. In both cases, add water to the pots immediately. Taste the foods in the fresh pots. If they taste too scorched, usually the only solution is to throw them out and start over.

Burned (in the frying pan)

If the cutlets have turned black as a hockey puck in the pan, it is best to go to the Italian restaurant next door.

The oil is too hot

If the oil or frying fat in the pan has become too hot and is already smoking, don't use it any more. Wipe out the cooled fat with paper towels and then wash the pan.

Lumps in the sauce

If there a few lumps, it helps to strain the sauce or gravy through a fine sieve. With many lumps, work on the sauce with a hand mixer and then strain it through the sieve.

Measuring the Quantities

Practical beyond measure—the most commonly used abbreviations for the measured quantities that you find in every cookbook:	
pound (lb)	1 lb = 16 oz
ounce (oz)	16 oz = 1 lb
gallon (gal)	1 gal = 3.78 l
liter (l)	1 l = 1.05 qt
quart (qt)	1 qt = 2 pt
pint (pt)	1 pt = 2 cups = 16 fl oz
cup	1 cup = 16 Tbsp = 8 fl oz
fluid ounce (fl oz)	1 fl oz = 2 Tbsp
tablespoon (Tbsp)	1 Tbsp = 3 tsp
teaspoon (tsp)	

Other Useful Terms	
knife point	amount that fits on the tip of a paring knife
pinch	amount that fits between thumb and forefinger
bunch	several stalks or sprigs of a fresh herb
heaping	a quantity of an ingredient that piles up above the confines of its measuring vessel
leveled	a heaping amount that has been scraped level with the top of the measuring vessel (usually with the back of a butter knife)

MIGHTY max

Preparation:

1. Halve the peppers, remove the white inner membrane and seeds and wash. Lay them on a sheet and bake on the highest rack in the oven for 10-15 minutes at 400°F (200° C). When the skin begins to blister, take the pepper halves out of the oven, remove the skin, and cut into strips. Peel the onions and cut them into strips.

2. Stir a sauce of salt, pepper, vinegar, and oil and pour over the pepper and onion strips. Wash the basil leaves, shake dry, and cut small.

3. Wash the pearl onions, dry, and cut into fine, round slices. Cube the ham. Heat half the clarified butter in the pan and brown the onions and ham cubes. Spread butter on the bread slices and distribute the browned ham cubes on the bread.

4. Heat the rest of the clarified butter in a pan. Carefully crack the eggs into a cup, one after the other, and make sure they are fresh. Let each egg slide into the pan by itself and fry over low heat. When the egg white is firm and white, sprinkle salt and pepper on the edge. The yolk should remain soft. Carefully take the fried eggs out of the pan and slide them onto the ham on the bread. Garnish the egg yolks with the basil. Add the pepper salad to the plates.

Ingredients:

For the Max:	For the pepper salad:
4, $\frac{1}{3}$ lb (150g) slices of cooked ham	1 each yellow, red, and green peppers
8 fresh eggs	1 onion
4 slices of rye bread	salt and pepper
4 $\frac{1}{8}$ Tbsp (60g) clarified butter	1 Tbsp vinegar
3 $\frac{1}{2}$ Tbsp (50g) butter	2 Tbsp oil
4 pearl onions	Fresh basil
Salt and pepper	

PORK tenderloin
on Toast

Small, but nice | for 4 people | 25 minutes

Preparation:

1. Wash the pork fillet under cold running water, pat dry with paper towels, and slice into pieces about $^1/_2$ inch (1.5cm) thick. Beat them somewhat flat and pepper lightly. Wash the parsley, shake dry, and chop small. Wash the cherry tomatoes and let them dry.

2. Wash the field greens salad and let it dry. Peel the onions and dice small. For the salad dressing, mix the vinegar, salt, pepper, and oil. Add the dressing to the greens and toss to distribute.

3. Clean the mushrooms with a mushroom or kitchen brush. Do not wash them, as they absorb water and lose flavor! Really tough dirt can be cut away with a paring knife. Cut off the stems. Use only undamaged mushrooms. Cut them into slices.

4. Toast the bread and place on four plates, two pieces per plate. Heat the clarified butter in a pan and brown the fillet slices briefly on both sides. Salt and pepper lightly. Take the pork out of the pan and place in an oven set to warm (80° C). Sauté the mushroom slices with the butter in the same pan, and add the chopped parsley.

5. Put the fillets on the toast and add the mushrooms. Cut the Camembert into slices and place on top of four of the toasts. Put a slice of cheddar cheese on each of the other four toasts. Bake briefly at 425° F (220° C) in a preheated oven until the cheese melts.

6. Garnish with the cherry tomatoes and serve with the field greens salad.

Ingredients:

1 pork tenderloin fillet (1-1 ½ lbs [500-600g])	3 ¾ cups (250g) sliced mushrooms	For the field greens salad:
Salt and pepper	1 pinch of parsley	1, 8-oz bag of prepared field greens salad mix
1 ⅓ Tbsp (20g) butter	7 oz (200g) Camembert cheese	1 onion
3 ½ Tbsp (50g) clarified butter	4 slices of cheddar cheese	3 Tbsp each vinegar and oil
8 slices of toasting bread	12 cherry tomatoes	Salt and pepper

Meaty HERB croquettes

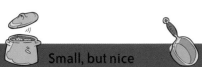

with Tsatsiki

Small, but nice · **for 4 people** · **60 minutes**

Ingredients:

1 roll
2 onions
1 bunch coriander
~1 lb (400g) mixed ground meat
1 Tbsp vegetable oil or fat
for frittering
(quantity depends on
amount to be frittered)
Iodized salt
Freshly ground pepper
Fresh mint leaves

For the Tsatsiki:

1 salad cucumber (300g)
2 cloves garlic
1 bunch fresh dill
1 ¼ cups (250g) Greek yogurt
2 Tbsp lemon juice
Iodized salt
Freshly ground pepper

Preparation:

1. Cube the roll and soften in 1 cup water. Peel the onions and chop fine. Wash the coriander, shake dry, and chop.

2. Press the roll well and knead with the ground meat, egg, onion pieces, and coriander. Flavor with salt and pepper.

3. Make balls of the ground meat mixture. Heat the vegetable oil to 325°F (170°C) degrees C in deep fryer or a large pot. Fry the meat balls until crisp (about 4 minutes each), remove, and place on a paper towel to drain.

4. Wash the salad cucumber, grate coarsely, and let dry. Peel the garlic and chop fine. Wash the dill, shake dry, and chop fine. Save a dill sprig to garnish the plate.

5. Mix the salad cucumber, garlic, and dill with the yogurt, and lemon juice. Season heavily with salt and pepper.

6. Pour the tsatsiki into a serving bowl and plate with the meatballs. Garnish with the remaining dill sprig and a few mint leaves. Baguettes or flatbread are a good accompaniment.

> Season the grated salad cucumber beforehand with salt and let dry. The salt will draw the moisture from the vegetable.

TOMATO soup
with Mozzarella

Small, but nice | **for 4 people** | **40 minutes**

Ingredients:

4-4 ½ ripe tomatoes (800g)
2 onions
1 clove garlic
1 small, mild pepper
2 Tbsp olive oil
3 ⅛ cups (750ml) vegetable broth
2 sprigs thyme
2 small sprigs parsley
1 small sprig rosemary
1 bay leaf
1 celery heart
1, 8 ⅞-oz package of basil mozzarella (250g)
Salt and pepper

For the Garnish:

Rosemary blossoms
Chive stalks

Preparation:

1. Wash the tomatoes, quarter, remove stem, and cut small. Peel the onions and garlic and dice both small. Halve the pepper lengthwise, remove stem, seeds, and inner membrane, then cut fine.

2. Heat the olive oil in a large pot and heat the onion cubes, garlic, and pepper in it. Add the tomato pieces and warm briefly. Stir in the vegetable broth and season with salt and pepper.

3. Add the herbs and the celery heart, bring to a boil, reduce heat, and simmer covered about 20 minutes. Take out the herbs and celery.

4. Strain the soup through a fine sieve and flavor again. Let the mozzarella drip very dry and cut into ⅛-inch (0.5cm) cubes.

5. Pour the soup into preheated cups and add the mozzarella cubes. Serve garnished with rosemary blossoms and chives.

> Sun-ripened tomatoes are simply unbeatable for this soup.

Savory CREAM OF PEA soup
with Trout

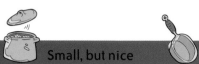 Small, but nice for 4 people 🕐 35 minutes

Ingredients:

³/₄ lb (350g) trout fillet
1 lime
1 onion
2 Tbsp (30g) butter
2 cups (300g) frozen peas
2 ¹/₂ cups (600ml) vegetable broth
⁷/₈ cup (200ml) white wine
⁷/₈ cup (200ml) sweet cream
3 Tbsp horseradish
1 bunch tarragon or parsley
Salt and pepper
Fresh sage

Preparation:

1. Wash the fish fillet under cold running water, pat dry with paper towels, and cube.

2. Wash the lime with hot water, pat dry, and squeeze out the juice. Add the lime juice and rind to the fish cubes and marinate covered.

3. Peel the onions and dice small. Heat the butter in a pot and sauté the onion cubes in it.

4. Add 1 ¹/₃ cup (200g) of peas to the onions in the pot and cook them briefly. Pour in the vegetable broth and wine, season with salt and pepper, and cook for about 8 minutes.

5. Beat the cream stiff and add the horseradish. Wash the tarragon or parsley, shake dry, and cut into thin strips.

6. Puree the pea soup, strain it through a sieve and heat it again. Then add the rest of the peas and the tarragon or parsley strips.

7. Poach the fish fillet cubes along with the lime juice and ³/₈ cup (100ml) of water in a pot for 2-3 minutes.

8. Add the fish cubes to the broth with the horseradish and cream. Note: Do not cook the soup any more! Flavor the soup, ladle into bowls, and garnish with some sage. You can serve warm baguettes with it.

DUMPLING soup
with Carrots and Savory Custard

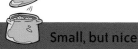

Small, but nice   for 4 people   60 minutes

Ingredients:

1, 1 lb bag of baby carrots (100g)
4 cups (1l) vegetable broth
Salt, pepper, and nutmeg

For the custard:

3 eggs
$^3/_4$ cup (180ml) whole milk
Salt, pepper, and nutmeg

For the dumplings:

$^1/_2$ bundle chives
$^3/_4$ cup (180ml) whole milk
$^1/_3$ Tbsp (5g) pure
Vegetable margarine
$^1/_3$ cup (60g) hard wheat grits
1 egg white
Salt, pepper, and nutmeg

Preparation:

1. Peel the carrots, halve them the long way and cook in lightly salted water until ready to eat. Wash the chives, shake dry, and chop fine, keeping a few for garnish.

2. Beat the eggs for the custard and stir in the milk. Season with salt, pepper, and nutmeg. Line a bowl with plastic wrap, pour in the egg mixture and bring to coagulation in a boiling water bath for 30 minutes. Then refrigerate, dump out, and cut into squares.

3. For the dumplings, bring the milk to a boil with margarine, salt, pepper, and nutmeg. Sprinkle in the grits and stir until the mixture loosens from the bottom of the pot. Put it directly into a bowl and stir in the egg yolk and chives.

4. Bring the vegetable broth to a boil and make dumplings of the cooled dumpling mixture with a teaspoon and a moistened hands. Cook 1 or 2 minutes in the broth and let stand for 10 minutes.

5. Add the custard and carrots to the soup, season with salt, pepper, and nutmeg, and add the remaining chives to the soup. Serve the soup in one big tureen or deep bowls.

RUMP steak
with Chanterelles

Small, but nice | for 4 people | 25 minutes prep + 1 hour cooking time

Ingredients:

4 rump steaks, each $1/2$ lb (250g)

2 Tbsp clarified butter

$4^{2}/_{3}$ cups (400g) fresh chanterelle mushrooms

1 onion

~ $1/2$ cup (100g) butter

$1/2$ bunch chives

Salt and pepper

1 package cherry tomatoes

French bread

Preparation:

1. Wash the rump steaks under cold running water and pat dry with paper towels.

2. Preheat the oven to 175°F (80°C) and warm a fire-resistant roasting pan in it.

3. Heat the clarified butter in a frying pan and brown the steaks on high heat for about 2 minutes on each side.

4. Lay the steaks in the preheated roasting pan and season both sides with salt and pepper. Roast in the preheated oven for an hour. The steaks can stay in the oven problem-free for another half hour.

5. Clean the chanterelles with a mushroom or kitchen brush. Do not wash them, since they soon absorb water and lose flavor! Very stubborn dirt can be cut away with a paring knife. Cut off the stems. Use only undamaged mushrooms.

6. Peel the onion and cut into small cubes. Melt the butter in a pan and caramelize the onions on low temperature until translucent. Add the chanterelles and cook for 5 minutes.

7. Wash the chives, shake dry, and cut fine.

8. Season the chanterelles with salt and pepper and stir in the chives shortly before serving. Arrange the rump steaks on plates with the chanterelles and a few washed cherry tomatoes. Serve with the French bread.

> In the drippings that remain in the roasting pan, cook the onion cubes until translucent. Stir in 2 cups ($1/2$ l) water and 1 Tbsp of instant roasting sauce with a whisk. Finally, add the cream and season to taste.

They can also come from a can! It goes much faster but doesn't look as good.

16

> With side dishes like potatoes or vegetables, make the rump steak portions a little smaller and shorten the cooking time accordingly.

17

CHEESE spätzle

  Small, but nice for 4 people 60 minutes

Ingredients:

5 cups (500g) flour
5 large eggs
2 cups (200g) grated Swiss cheese
1 ½ cups (50g) cooking fat
1 large onion

Preparation:

1. Sift the flour into a bowl, beat in the eggs, and stir thoroughly with a stirring spoon until the dough forms bubbles. The stirring is important—better too much than too little. So never use a hand whisk or the whisk from a hand mixer! When you lift the spoon and the dough no longer moves, it is ready.

2. Bring plenty of salted water to a boil in a big pot. Put 1-2 tablespoons of dough on a wet board, cut into thin strips with a knife dipped in water, and then drop the very fine, even strips into the boiling water. Keep dipping the knife into cold water so the dough will not stick to it.

3. The noodles are finished when they float on the surface. Take them out with a slotted spoon and put them aside to dry.

4. Peel the onion, cut into fine cubes, and brown in cooking fat.

5. Make alternating layers of noodles and grated cheese in a casserole dish, with a layer of cheese on top. Scatter the fried onion over the top and bake for about 15-20 minutes in an oven preheated to 350°F (180°C).

> A fresh green salad or cucumber salad accompanies this dish nicely.
> Or applesauce for those with a sweet tooth.

BLUEBERRY pancakes
with Vanilla Ice Cream and Angel's Hair

Small, but nice • for 4 people • 45 minutes

Ingredients:

2 Tbsp (30g) butter

2 eggs

$^7/_8$ cup (80g) flour

$^1/_2$ cup (120ml) milk

1 pinch salt

$^1/_2$ cup (100g) sugar

Some butter for baking

2 $^2/_3$ Tbsp (40ml) currant liqueur

1 star anise

2 cups (300g) blueberries

$^1/_2$ tsp corn starch

$^7/_8$ cup (100g) sour cream

4 scoops vanilla ice cream

Confectioners' sugar

For the angel hair:

~ $^1/_2$ cup (80g) sugar

1 $^1/_8$ Tbsp (25g) glucose

$^1/_2$ tsp cinnamon

Preparation:

1. Melt the butter in a small pot; it may turn light brown. Mix the butter with the eggs, sifted flour, milk, salt, and 1 $^1/_2$ tablespoons sugar to a smooth dough. Let it rise 20 minutes and perhaps add some mineral water. In a large coated frying pan, with a little butter, cook 4 thin pancakes one after another. Put the oven on warm and place the pancakes on a plate in the oven to keep them warm.

2. Caramelize—cook slowly on medium heat in a clean dry pan—the rest of the sugar with the currant liqueur and anise star in a pan. Add the blueberries and cook for 5 minutes, until most of berries have burst. Bind lightly with the starch and let it cool.

3. For the angel hair, caramelize the sugar and glucose with 1 $^1/_2$ tablespoons of water until the mixture is a light golden brown (~285°F [142°C]). Cool the bottom of the pot briefly in cold water and stir in the cinnamon. Drizzle the caramel over a cooking spoon with a tablespoon to create fine strands of sugar. Lift the cooking spoon and detach the angel hair.

4. Mix the sour cream with the berries. Put a dollop of blueberries and sour cream in the middle of each pancake and fold it into a triangle. Plate the pancakes and add a scoop of vanilla ice cream and some angel hair on each. Dust with confectioners' sugar and serve immediately.

BAVARIAN crème
with Blueberries

Small, but nice | for 8 people | 35 minutes + 2 Hours for chilling

Ingredients:

For the crème:

1 genuine bourbon vanilla pod in a glass jar
1 cup ($^1/_4$ l) milk
4 egg yolks
$^3/_4$ cup (100g) sifted confectioners' sugar
6 sheets white gelatin
2 cups ($^1/_2$ l) sweet cream

For the blueberry sauce:

2 $^3/_4$ cups (400g) blueberries
3 $^1/_3$ Tbsp (50ml) white wine
2 Tbsp sugar
$^1/_2$-1 Tbsp cinnamon

For the garnish:

Fresh mint leaves
Some cinnamon

Strawberries work well also!

Preparation:

1. Cut the vanilla pod open lengthwise, scrape out the seeds, and cook both pod and seeds with the milk.

2. Stir the egg yolks with the sifted confectioners' sugar to a froth in a hot water bath.

3. Take the vanilla pod out of the milk. Slowly stir the milk into the egg mixture until it thickens. This is the base for the crème.

4. Soften the gelatin in cold water following the instructions on the package, dissolve, and pour into the crème.

5. Beat the cream stiff and mix into the crème when it begins to gel. Put into eight forms or custard dishes and refrigerate about an hour.

6. Pick over the blueberries and wash if needed. Save a few berries for garnish. Puree the rest with the white wine and sugar, and flavor with the cinnamon.

7. Turn the crèmes over onto plates and serve with the blueberry sauce. Garnish with the remaining blueberries and mint leaves, and dust with some cinnamon.

COOKING school

Cooking Techniques from A to Z

Carve
To cut serving portions from a cooked protein such as roast beef, pork loin, or poultry.

Clean
Removing unwanted or inedible parts from a protein (i.e. fish, beef, or fowl) such as offal, tendons, skin, or fat before preparation. These bits can be used for stock, however.

Cold Water Bath
Use a bath of cold water to immediately stop the cooking process. For example, placing eggs in a cold water bath directly from the pan makes them easier to shell. Also, vegetables retain their color, flavor, and texture when placed in a cold water bath to stop them from cooking.

Cook off
Using heat to cook the fat out of meat, bacon, for example.

Deep-fry
Cooking food by immersing it completely in heated cooking oil or fat. The key is to get the oil temperature high enough (275-375°F [140-190°C]) so a crisp crust forms around the food.

Al Dente
A toothsome texture, usually used to describe noodles, beans, or grains that are still a little firm, but ready to eat.

Bacon-wrap
Wrapping low-fat meats with strips of bacon to prevent the meat from drying out. Usually the bacon is held on with a toothpick.

Baste
To pour meat drippings mixed with a little broth over roasting meat or vegetables.

Bind
To make a sauce, soup, or vegetable dish thicken by adding flour or starch. Stir flour into cold water until there are no clumps, then pour into the cooking liquid and continue to cook while stirring constantly.

Blanch
Briefly cooking vegetables or other food in boiling salt water and then immediately placing them in a cold water bath.

Bread
Coating ingredients successively with flour, beaten egg , and bread-crumbs before deep-frying, baking, or roasting.

Broil
A fast way to cook tender meats using a direct heat source that is above the food.

Flambé

To add the aroma of a liqueur or alcohol to food. Pour alcohol with at least 50% alcohol by volume (brandy, rum, or liqueur) into the dish you are cooking. Light the alcohol on fire with a match and let it cook off.

Fold In

Carefully adding beaten egg whites into a batter without stirring so the egg whites retain the air you have beaten into them. After adding the whites, use a spatula to cut a path down the middle of the mixture and gently fold one half of the mixture onto the other half. Only continue long enough to incorporate the whites and never use an electric mixer.

Gratin

Using very high heat (400-480°F [200-250°C]) to make a light crust on top of a casserole with breadcrumbs, cheese, butter, or egg.

Grill

Cooking food at high temperature with the direct heat of an open flame.

Marinate

Soaking fish or meat in a liquid enriched with herbs and spices for several hours.

Roux

A mixture of wheat flour and fat or butter used for thickening soups or sauces (such as a Béchamel sauce). The degree to which the butter is browned gives a white, blond, or brown result. Melt butter in a pot and add flour, stirring constantly, then add it to the liquid to be thickened.

Separate eggs

Carefully strike the middle of the long axis of an egg on the edge of a firm vessel. Hold the egg over the vessel and carefully break it apart at the crack. Ideally two equal halves will result and part of the egg white will flow into the vessel. Separate the rest of the whites by repeatedly pouring the contents of the half with the yolk into the empty half.

Sift

To pass through a fine sieve.

Simmer

Cooking vegetables over low heat with little fat and liquid, without browning.

Stew

Cooking ingredients in a covered pot in the oven or on the stove with reduced liquid and little fat.

Stock

Liquid that remains in a pot when fish, meat, or vegetables are cooked, roasted, steamed, or simmered. It is the best base for a sauce.

Thicken

See also "bind." To thicken with an egg yolk, add the yolk to a small bowl of stock or sauce from the food you are cooking. Be careful not to get egg shell in the liquid. Stir the yolk with the stock and then pour the mixture into the sauce or soup and remove the dish from heat.

SCRAMBLED pancakes
Two Ways*

Simple menu   for 4 people   45 minutes to cook + 2 hours to infuse flavors

Preparation:

1. Wash the raisins with hot water and soften them in the rum for about 2 hours.

2. Peel, core, and cut up the apples for the applesauce. Put into a pot with 1 1/4 cup (300ml) water, the lemon juice, and sugar. For very sour apples, use a little more sugar. Bring it to a boil and let the apples soften over low heat. Work into applesauce with a hand mixer.

3. Separate the eggs and beat the yolks to a froth with the sugar. Then mix in the salt and cream.

4. Beat the egg white stiff, add the sugar and cream mixture, and carefully fold in the flour.

5. Melt half the butter in a pan, put in half the dough, and stir smooth. Cook 4-5 minutes over low heat until the bottom is lightly browned. Then flip the pancake over and fry golden brown on the other side. Cut into bite-size pieces with a wooden spatula.

6. Melt the rest of the butter in a pan for the other half of the dough, put the dough in with the raisins, stir smooth, and prepare the second pancake as in Step 5.

7. Arrange the pieces on plates and dust with confectioners' sugar. Serve with the applesauce.

* These sugared pancakes are a traditional dessert from Austria and Bavaria. In German they are called Kaiserschmarrn, which translates as "Emperor's rubbish."

Ingredients:

2 ⁷/₈ cups (280g) flour	1 Tbsp butter	**For the applesauce:**
¹/₂ cup (80g) sugar	²/₃ cup (100g) raisins	3 ¹/₃ lbs (1 ¹/₂ kg) apples
4 pinches salt	1 ²/₃ Tbsp (25ml) rum	5 Tbsp sugar
2 cups (500ml) sweet cream	Confectioners' sugar	1 Tbsp lemon juice
12 medium eggs		

> To beat egg whites stiff, the bowl and beaters can't have any fat on them, and there can't be any yolk in the egg white.
> Egg whites take on a better consistency when a pinch of salt is added before beating.

HAM and TOMATO noodles

  Simple menu for 4 people 30 minutes

Preparation:

1. Cook the noodles according to the directions on the package. When they are still a little toothsome, drain them, divide them into two halves, and let them drip dry.

2. Mix the eggs with salt and pepper. Note: Season carefully, as the ham already has a lot of flavor!

3. Wash the chives, shake them dry, and cut fine. Wash the cherry tomatoes and let them dry.

4. Cut the lettuce leaves off the stem, wash them, cut them into bite-size pieces for the salad, and let them dry in a colander. Peel the onion and cut into small cubes. Mix a salad dressing of the salt, pepper, sugar, lemon juice, balsamic vinegar, and olive oil.

5. Melt some clarified butter in a pan, sauté the ham cubes, and add half the noodles. Pour half the beaten eggs over the noodles and fry them, stirring constantly with a wooden spatula.

6. Melt the rest of the clarified butter in a pan for the other half of the noodles, cook the cherry tomatoes briefly and add the rest of the noodles. Pour the rest of the eggs over the noodles and fry, stirring constantly with a wooden spatula. Then flavor the noodles somewhat.

7. Pour salad dressing over the salad shortly before serving, and put into bowls.

8. Scatter the chives liberally over the noodles, and serve with the salad.

Ingredients:	For the salad:
1, 1-lb package of noodles (500g)	1 head of red leaf lettuce
1 Tbsp clarified butter	1 Tbsp balsamic vinegar
1/3 lb (150g) mildly spiced, cubed ham	1 Tbsp olive oil
2 cups (300g) cherry tomatoes	1 onion
4 eggs	Salt and pepper
Salt and pepper	Sugar
1 bunch of chives	Juice of half a lemon

POTATOES au gratin
with Harzer* Sauce

Simple menu   for 6 people   25 minutes prep + 25 minutes for baking

Ingredients:

1 ²/₃ lbs (750g) potatoes
1 small zucchini
3 onions
2 Tbsp butter or margarine
1 tsp instant vegetable broth
1 cup (125g) light sour cream
8 ⁷/₈ oz (250g) Harzer cheese
¹/₂ cup (125ml) sweet cream
Grease for the pan
Salt and pepper
Ground nutmeg

Preparation:

1. Wash the potatoes, peel them, and cut them into thin slices ¹/₈ inch (3-4mm) thick. Put them in salt water and bring to a boil. Let them cook in a covered pot about 5 minutes, pour off the water, and let them drip dry.

2. Wash the zucchini, remove bad spots, the stem, and blossom, and cut it too into thin slices.

3. Peel the onions and cut into fine cubes. Melt the butter or margarine in a pan and sauté the onions until translucent. Note: Don't let the butter get too hot, or it will burn quickly!

4. Preheat the oven to 400°F (200°C).

5. Mix the instant vegetable broth into 1 cup (¹/₄ l) hot water. Season with salt, pepper, and nutmeg. Add the light sour cream, heat the mixture, and melt the Harzer cheese in it. Then add the cream.

6. Grease a casserole pan, lay the potato slices in it and distribute the zucchini slices among them.

7. Distribute the sautéd onion cubes over them and cover with the prepared gratin sauce. Bake about 25 minutes in the preheated oven and serve.

*Harzer cheese is a German sour milk cheese from the Harz Mountains. It is made from low-fat curd cheese and is known for its strong flavor. Limburger is a suitable substitute if Harzer is not available.

POTATO pancakes
with Chivey Cottage Cheese

Ingredients:

2 1/4 lbs (1kg) potatoes

1 egg

3 Tbsp flour

1/2 tsp salt

Ground nutmeg

8 Tbsp sunflower oil

2 1/8 cups (500g) light cottage cheese

1/2 tsp cumin

1 grated onion

2 Tbsp chives finely cut

Pepper

Preparation:

1. Peel the potatoes, grate them coarsely, put them into a sieve, and press out well. Pour off the potato water that comes out.

2. Mix the egg, flour, and salt into the grated potato and season with nutmeg. Form flat pancakes of the dough and fry them crisp in 6 tablespoons of heated oil.

3. Mix the cottage cheese with the remaining oil to a creamy texture. Fold in the cumin, onions, and chives and season well with salt and pepper. Serve the potato puffs with the cottage cheese and chives.

MEAT patties
with potato salad

Simple menu   for 4 people   50 minutes

Ingredients:

1 ⅓ lbs (600g) mixed ground meat
1 stale roll
2 eggs
2 onions
½ clove garlic
Salt and pepper
Ground nutmeg
1 bunch parsley
1 tsp marjoram
½ tsp paprika
2 ¾ Tbsp (40g) clarified butter
2 ¼ lbs (1kg) firm cooking potatoes
Vinegar
Vegetable oil
~1 cup (¼ l) vegetable broth

Preparation:

1. Boil the unpeeled potatoes about 20 minutes, then peel and cut into slices. Peel the onions and garlic and cut into fine cubes. Wash the parsley, shake dry, and chop fine.

2. Mix a vinaigrette of the warm vegetable broth, salt, pepper, vinegar, oil, and half the onion cubes and parsley. Pour it over the potato slices and mix well.

3. Soften the roll a few minutes in warm water and squeeze it out well.

4. Put the ground meat, eggs, and roll in a bowl. Melt 2 teaspoons of clarified butter, sauté the garlic cubes and the rest of the onion cubes and add to the ground meat. Season with salt, pepper, nutmeg, marjoram, and paprika powder. Add the rest of the parsley and knead the ground meat well.

5. From the meat make meat patties and fry them brown in the rest of the heated clarified butter. Plate the meat with the potato salad and serve.

Important!!!
Definitely use firm cooking potatoes.
Otherwise the salad will be messy.

> For the potato salad, use similarly sized potatoes so all are cooked at the same time.
> Salad variations: wash radishes, cut into slices, and mix into the salad.
> White bread can be substituted for the stale roll.

MUNICH Schnitzel
with Potato and Cucumber Salad

Simple menu · for 4 people · 50 minutes

Ingredients:

8 small pork tenderloin cutlets
4 Tbsp sweet mustard
Salt and pepper
$^1/_2$ cup (50g) flour
$^7/_8$ cup (100g) breadcrumbs
2 eggs
$^1/_3$ cup (100g) clarified butter
2 $^1/_4$ lbs (1kg) firm cooking potatoes
1 onion
1 cup ($^1/_4$ l) vegetable broth
$^1/_2$ salad cucumber
Cocktail tomatoes
$^1/_2$ bunch parsley
Vinegar and vegetable oil

Preparation:

1. Boil the unpeeled potatoes about 20 minutes, then peel and cut into slices while warm. Peel the cucumber, quarter, and slice. Add it to the potatoes, saving a few slices for decoration. Peel the onion and cut into fine cubes. Wash the parsley, shake dry, and chop fine.

2. Mix a vinaigrette of the warm vegetable broth, salt, pepper, vinegar, oil, onion, and parsley; pour it over the salad. Mix everything well. Garnish with the remaining cucumber slices and a few tomatoes.

3. Wash the cutlets in cold water, pat dry with paper towels, season on both sides with salt and pepper, and coat with sweet mustard. Beat the eggs in a small bowl and put the flour and breadcrumbs on separate plates. Dip both sides of the cutlets in the flour, drag through the eggs, and then coat with breadcrumbs.

4. Melt the clarified butter in a pan and fry the cutlets one at a time until golden brown on each side (~4-5 minutes). Take the cutlets out, place on paper towels, and place in the oven on warm.

5. Plate the cutlets and serve with the potato cucumber salad.

CHINESE stir-fry
with Salmon Fillet

Ingredients:

1 ¹/₃ lbs (600g) salmon fillet
1 red and 1 yellow pepper
¹/₂ lb (250g) soybean sprouts
1 ¹/₂ cups (150g) fresh shiitake or champignons mushrooms
2 Tbsp oil
8 Tbsp sweet chili sauce
³/₈ cup (100ml) vegetable broth
Salt

For the marinade:

1 clove garlic
1 lemon
2 Tbsp honey
8 Tbsp soy sauce

Preparation:

1. Wash the salmon fillet under cold running water, pat dry with paper towels, and cut into crude chunks.

2. Peel the garlic and cut into fine cubes. Press the lemon. Mix the honey, lemon juice, soy sauce, and garlic cubes. Marinate the salmon fillet in it for 20 minutes.

3. Halve the peppers, remove the membranes and seeds, wash, and cut small. Wash the soybean shoots and let drip dry.

4. Clean the mushrooms with a mushroom or kitchen brush. Don't wash them in water; they absorb too much water and will lose flavor! Very stubborn dirt can be cut away with a paring knife. Cut off the stems and halve the mushrooms. Use only undamaged mushrooms.

5. Take the salmon out of the marinade and let it drip dry. Keep the marinade. Heat the oil in a coated pan. Sauté the salmon in hot oil for about 2 minutes. Take out and keep warm.

6. Fry the peppers and mushrooms on high heat; add the marinade, chili sauce, and vegetable broth. Heat for 2 minutes, then add the soy sprouts and pieces of salmon fillet. Season with salt and heat briefly again. Serve in bowls.

spicy CUBAN stir-fry

Ingredients:

1 ⅛ lbs (500g) pork loin
1 large green zucchini and
1 yellow zucchini
1 red onion
4 pearl onions
1 large banana
2 Tbsp oil
⅞ cup (200ml) coconut milk
⅜ cup (100ml) white wine
Salt
1 tsp curry powder
½ tsp sweet mild pepper
¼ tsp Cayenne pepper

Preparation:

1. Wash the pork in cold water, pat dry, and cut into strips. Wash the zucchini, cut lengthwise into eighths, and then into strips. Peel the onion and cut into rings. Wash the pearl onions and cut lengthwise into pieces about ¾ inch (2cm) long. Peel the banana and cut into slices.

2. Fry the pork slices in hot oil. Add the zucchini strips and onion rings and fry about 5 minutes. Pour in the coconut milk, vegetable broth, and wine; bring to a boil and then reduce to a simmer for 8-10 minutes. Mix in the pearl onions. Season with salt, curry powder, paprika, and Cayenne, then add the banana slices.

Colorful
COWBOY griddle

  Simple menu for 4 people 45 minutes

Preparation:

1. For the barbecue sauce, wash the beefsteak tomatoes, quarter them, remove the stems, and cut into cubes. Heat the oil and simmer the tomato cubes and garlic in it for 5 minutes. Puree the sauce and season with the honey, vinegar, chili flakes, and salt.

2. Wash the potatoes, peel them, cut into strips, and fry to a golden brown in a pan with heated oil for about 20-25 minutes. Take out the potatoes and keep them warm. Peel the onions and cut into rings. Halve the peppers, remove the membrane and seeds, wash and cube.

3. Wash the steaks in cold water, pat dry, cut into strips, and fry in the fat leftover from the potatoes. Add the onion rings, garlic, and pepper cubes. Let the kidney beans drip dry, add them to the warm potatoes, and heat briefly. Flavor the cowboy dish with salt and steak seasoning and serve with the barbecue sauce.

Ingredients:

For the barbecue sauce:	For the potato dish:
4 beefsteak tomatoes	1 $^1/_3$ lbs (600g) potatoes
2 tsp cooking oil	2 Tbsp cooking oil
1 large clove garlic	2 onions
4 Tbsp honey	1 red, 1 green, and 1 yellow pepper
2 tsp medium-strength vinegar	1 $^1/_8$ lbs (500g) beefsteak
2-4 cups ($^1/_2$ - 1l) chili flakes	1 medium clove garlic
Salt	1, 16-oz can kidney beans
	Salt
	3-4 tsp steak seasoning

TUNA FISH pasta
"Diavolo"

Simple menu | for 2 people | 25 minutes

Ingredients:

5 ¼ oz (150g) spaghetti
5 cups (100g) arugula
2 red peppers (hot)
¼ cup (50g) grated Parmesan cheese
1, 6-oz can of tuna with garlic

Preparation:

1. Cook the spaghetti according to the package. When it is still toothsome, drain it and let it drip dry.

2. Wash the arugula, remove the stems, and chop the leaves coarsely.

3. Cut the pepper in rings and grate the Parmesan coarsely.

4. Flake apart the tuna in a bowl using a fork. Mix in the spaghetti and pepper rings.

5. Serve the tuna pasta sprinkled with Parmesan and arugula.

PENNE à L'arrabiata

 Simple menu for 4 people ⏱ 50 minutes

Ingredients:

~ 4 large tomatoes (750g)
1 small onion
4 cloves garlic
1-2 red peppers (hot)*
2 Tbsp olive oil
4 ³/₄ cups (500g) penne
¹/₂ bunch basil
¹/₄ cup (50g) grated hard cheese

(Note: spice levels can vary depending on the type!)

Preparation:

1. Peel the tomatoes, remove the stems, and cut an "X" into the skin on the bottom. Pour boiling water over the tomatoes. When the cut skin rolls, take the tomatoes out of the water and chill in a cold water bath. Now you can simply pull off the skin with a sharp knife and cut the pulp into cubes.

2. Peel the onion and garlic. Dice the onion and chop the garlic. Wash and finely chop the pepper.

3. Heat the olive oil and caramelize the onion, garlic, and pepper pieces. Add the tomato cubes and salt; simmer for 20-30 minutes.

4. Cook the noodles according to the directions on the package until ready to eat. Wash the basil, shake dry, and cut fine.

5. Do not rinse the noodles after draining them, but mix immediately with the sauce and basil. The residual heat of the noodle warms the sauce and infuses the flavor in the noodles. Plate the noodles and sauce, sprinkle the hard cheese over them, and serve.

Why is it always me???

Grit CAKES
with Plum sauce

  Simple menu for 4 people 🕐 40 minutes

Ingredients:

For the cakes:

$^7/_8$ cup (200ml) milk
$^1/_3$ cup (50g) yellow grits (powder)
2 Tbsp vanilla sugar
1 pinch salt
$^1/_2$ cup (100g) low-fat cream cheese

For the sauce:

1 $^7/_8$ cups (300g) sliced plums
$^2/_3$ cup (150ml) dry red wine
4 Tbsp sugar
$^1/_2$ tsp cinnamon

Plus:

Butter for frying
Confectioners' sugar
2 Tbsp almonds
Fresh lemon balm

Preparation:

1. Heat the milk and grits and sprinkle the vanilla sugar in. Add the salt, stir, and bring to a boil. Take the pot off the stove and let the grits rise. Stir in the cream cheese.

2. Wash the plums, pit, and cut into slices. Heat the red wine with the sugar and cinnamon. Reduce the heat, add the plums, and cook about 5 minutes.

3. Melt the butter in a pan, make about 12 round rolls out of the grits and fry to a golden brown on both sides.

4. Plate the grit cakes with the plum sauce and sprinkle with confectioners' sugar and almonds. Serve garnished with lemon balm or mint.

sweet PANcakes
with Apple Compote

 Simple menu for 4 people 25 minutes

Ingredients:

1 apple

Juice of 1 lemon

$^7/_8$ cup (200g) applesauce

$^1/_4$ cup (75g) caramel-flavored syrup

1 $^1/_2$ cups (150g) flour

2 eggs

$^1/_2$ cup (125ml) milk

1 pinch salt

2 Tbsp cooking oil

For the garnish:

Sweet cream

Currants

Grated chocolate

Fresh herb sprigs

Confectioners' sugar

Preparation:

1. Wash the apples, cut off the tops, and remove cores. Hollow the apples out slightly and drip lemon juice on them so they don't turn brown.

2. Mix the applesauce with the syrup, pour it into the apples, and put the tops back on.

3. Mix the flour, eggs, milk, and salt. Heat the oil in a pan and make thin pancakes. Roll them up and put them on plates.

4. Garnish the pancakes with whipped cream, currants, grated chocolate, and herb sprigs. Serve sprinkled with confectioners' sugar alongside the stuffed apples.

COOKING school

Knowledge for show-offs

Theoretically, you have learned a thing or two in the first two lessons. If you'd like to impress people with your culinary knowledge, here are some well-kept secrets and tips about various foods.

How much **calf liver** should go into calf liverwurst? The answer will amaze you: None! Liver, to be sure, must be included, but its strictly pig liver. Of course liverwurst must also have veal in it.

Don't be deceived by the term **"cholesterol-free" cooking oil**. Almost all vegetable oils (rapeseed oil, sunflower oil, etc.) naturally have little to no cholesterol!

Who would not think of **grain bread as whole-grain**? By the legal definition, whole-grain bread is only that which contains at least 90% whole-grain flour. Many breads and rolls are available that use dark coloring and decorative grains to fool you with their whole-grain look.

Does **nectar** make you think of nature, bees, honey? You're way off—nectar is a mixture of fruit juice, water, and sugar. The fruit amounts to between 25% and 50%, and the sugar content is high!

If you think **German caviar** comes from sturgeon caught in German waters, you're fooling yourself. It is merely roe from lumpfish caught off Iceland that has been colored and aroma-enhanced.

Unhandled lemons have not been treated on the surface since being picked. That much is true. But to assume that an unhandled lemon is completely organic would be going too far. The use of fertilizers and pesticides in growing is not ruled out!

The **Munich white sausage** is the pride of Bavaria, but the raw materials for the sausage can come from all over the world.

Smoothies are fashionable and very tasty, but pureed fruit mixed with juice cannot replace fresh fruit in your daily diet.

Think of delicious **smoked sausage,** prepared in the smoker directly over wood … but be careful, the meat may also have been drenched with industrial liquid smoke. Look for products without additives.

Bavarian liver cheese must not be taken literally; as a rule it contains no liver, and it doesn't have to be Bavarian either.

Alcohol-free beer seems alcohol-free at first, but it isn't! It can contain up to 0.5% alcohol. Cheers!

→ It is best to taste sauerkraut before cooking with it. Wash it with cold water if necessary. If it is still too sour, you can balance the flavor with some hot apple cider.

→ Carefully blanch carrots in butter, so they will keep their bright orange color. With too much heat the vegetable soon browns because of its high sugar content.

→ Stale rolls or bread can be cubed and fried in butter to make croutons. They can then be used in cream soups or with vegetables. They not only taste good, but also look good. Your eyes, after all, eat along with you.

→ Fresh mushrooms stay lighter if you simmer them for about 10 minutes in some dry white wine.

→ Roasted potatoes become a nice golden brown and crispy when you scatter a few breadcrumbs over them.

→ Clean fresh strawberries only after washing them so they don't get watery. Let them stand covered at room temperature for an hour, covered and sprinkled with sugar, and their full aroma will unfold.

→ Any sauce can be thickened with a roux, but it must not be put directly into the boiling liquid. Instead, knead 1 3/4 tablespoons (25g) of butter and 1/3 cup (30g) of flour together and gradually add it to the sauce in small amounts until the sauce reaches the desired consistency.

→ A good preparation for beef is to boil it in lightly salted water. This keeps the meat nice and juicy. To make a good meat broth, put the cooked piece of meat in cold salted water for a little bit.

→ Eggs are best stored in a closed container in the refrigerator with their points downward. The porous shell quickly picks up smells, so never store eggs near cheese.

→ Garlic develops its full aroma when it is pressed instead of chopped. Caution: it must not be fried too hot or it will turn bitter!

→ When you make mashed potatoes, never used a hand mixer or beater. These tools will make the mixture too fine and turn the potatoes into a sticky paste.

Baked
PORK tenderloin

 **A little more effort** for 4 people | 20 minutes prep + 30 minutes to bake

Preparation:

1. Preheat the oven to 400°F (200°C).

2. Wash the pork loin under cold running water and pat dry with paper towels. Cut it into six equally large pieces, brown it unseasoned in the melted clarified butter, and place in a casserole dish.

3. Peel the onions and garlic cloves. Cut the onions into slices and press the garlic in a garlic press.

4. Caramelize the onion slices to a golden brown in the hot clarified butter and then add the garlic cloves and brown them. Pour in the cream and the double cream and season with salt and pepper. Let it cool somewhat.

5. Wash the parsley, shake dry, and cut small. Keep a heaping tablespoon of it for a garnish and mix the rest into the onions and cream.

6. Pour the sauce over the loin, sprinkle the grated cheese and the remaining parsley over it, and bake in the oven about 30 minutes.

7. Wash the tomatoes, cut into eighths, and put in a big salad bowl. Peel the onions and chop small.

8. Wash the parsley, shake dry, and cut small. Prepare a salad dressing from the spices, parsley, chopped onions, vinegar, and oil and pour over the tomatoes. Serve the baked pork loin with the tomato salad.

Ingredients:

For the pork tenderloin:	For the tomato salad:
1 pork tenderloin (~1 $\frac{1}{8}$ lbs [500g])	1 $\frac{3}{4}$ lbs (800g) tomatoes
5 onions	1 small onion
1 clove garlic	Salt, pepper, and some sugar
2 bunches of parsley	1 bunch parsley
$\frac{7}{8}$ cup (200ml) sweet cream	1 Tbsp balsamic vinegar
$\frac{1}{2}$ cup (125ml) double cream	6 Tbsp oil
1 $\frac{1}{8}$ cups (200g) grated cheese	
3 $\frac{1}{2}$ Tbsp (50g) clarified butter	
Salt and pepper	

> Serve French bread with this dish.
> The salad can basically be served right away, but it tastes much better if it sits seasoned at room temperature for at least an hour.

BEEF roulade

A little more effort — for 6 people — 50 minutes prep + 4 hours to cook

Preparation:

1. Preheat the oven to 215°F (100°C) and warm a tempered glass dish in it. Wash the beef fillets under cold running water and pat dry with paper towels. Halve the pepper, remove the membrane and seeds, and wash it. Cut one half into thin strips. Cut the pickles into long strips.

2. Spread out the rolls, sprinkle with salt and pepper, and spread with mustard. To 2/3 of each fillet add about 2/3 of the ham cubes, the pepper strips, and pickles. Carefully roll up the fillets so that the ingredients stay inside and tie with kitchen string.

3. Peel and cube the onions. Melt the clarified butter in a pan, brown the rolls for about 5 minutes, take them out and put them in the preheated dish. In the drippings from the pan, brown the onions and the rest of the ham cubes. Dice the other half of the pepper and add it to the pan along with the flour. Bring 4 cups (1l) water to a boil and dissolve the meat-stock powder in it. Add the onions and bring it to a boil.

4. Pour the sauce over the rolls in the glass dish and cover it. Cook for 3 hours at 215°F (100°C) on the middle rack of the oven and then another 30-40 minutes at 250°F (120°C). Turn the rolls in the sauce several times while cooking.

5. Meanwhile, remove the big leaves and stems from the kohlrabi. Peel the kohlrabi, quarter it, cut it into slices and then into fine strips. Melt the butter in a pan and add the kohlrabi strips. Add 2 tablespoons water and season with salt and pepper. Put a lid on the pot and steam the kohlrabi at a low temperature for 15-20 minutes. Wash the parsley, shake dry, and cut small. Cut the olives into slices.

6. After cooking, take the rolls out of the pot, put them on a tempered glass plate, remove the string, and put the plate in the warm oven. Warm the braising sauce and season with salt and pepper. Serve the rolls with the sauce and the kohlrabi dish.

> Salted potatoes accompany this dish nicely.
> Before serving, scatter the parsley over the potatoes and the olive rings over the kohlrabi.

Ingredients:

6 thin fillets of beef	For the kohlrabi vegetables:
2 pickles	3 kohlrabi
1 red pepper	2 $^3/_4$ Tbsp (40g) butter
$^2/_3$ lb (300g) ham (cubed)	Salt and pepper
Mustard	
3 $^1/_2$ Tbsp (50g) clarified butter	For the garnish:
3 onions	$^1/_2$ bunch parsley
4 tsp instant meat stock	$^1/_2$ cup (100g) chopped, pitted black olives
2 Tbsp instant roasting sauce	
1 Tbsp flour	
Salt and freshly ground pepper	
Kitchen string	

TUNA fish
with Basil and Potato Salad

Ingredients:

1, 6-oz can of tuna in olive oil
3 zucchinis
2 1/2 Tbsp (20g) pine nuts
8 firm cooking potatoes
1 bunch basil
3 Tbsp light balsamic vinegar
Salt and pepper

Preparation:

1. Open the tuna and drain the olive oil into a bowl.

2. Wash the zucchini, remove bad spots, stems, and blossoms, and cut lengthwise into long strips. Heat 2 tablespoons of the collected oil and fry the zucchini strips in it.

3. Briefly roast the pine nuts without oil. As soon as they are golden brown, take them out of the pan and put them on paper towels (they turn black otherwise).

4. Wash the potatoes and cook for about 20 minutes in salt water. Don't let them get too soft, or they will fall apart. Drain the potatoes and let the potatoes cool slightly. Peel the warm potatoes and cut into thin slices. Wash the basil, pat dry, and chop fine.

5. Mix the basil with the salt, pepper, vinegar, and 2 more tablespoons of the oil, and mix it with the potatoes.

6. Plate the potato salad with the zucchini and the tuna. Serve with the pine nuts sprinkled on top.

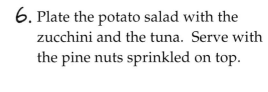

> Refine the dish with 2 tablespoons of diced olives.
> If you cook the potatoes the day before and keep the peels on, the pieces will not fall apart so easily and the salad looks better.

SALMON and gnocchi
with Mustard Sauce

A little more effort   for 4 people   35 minutes

Ingredients:

1 ⅓ lbs (600g) salmon fillet
1 large salad cucumber
1 onion
1 bunch parsley
2 Tbsp clarified butter
1 ¼ cups (300ml) vegetable broth
9 oz (250g) gnocchi
⅔ cup (150ml) medium-sharp mustard
2 Tbsp roux for a light sauce
Salt and pepper
Sugar

Preparation:

1. Wash the salmon fillet under cold running water, pat dry with paper towels, cut into crude cubes, and salt lightly.

2. Peel the cucumber, halve lengthwise, and cut into pieces. Peel and cube the onion. Wash the parsley, shake dry, and chop.

3. Melt a tablespoon of clarified butter in a pot and brown the onions and cucumber pieces in it. Pour the vegetable broth over it, add salt, pepper, and a pinch of sugar, and brown another 2-3 minutes.

4. Melt the rest of the clarified butter in a coated pan and brown the salmon pieces.

5. Cook the gnocchi according to the packaging, drain, and let drip dry.

6. Add the salmon, cream, and mustard to the vegetables and cook another 3 minutes.

7. Add the parsley, season the sauce, and thicken with the roux. Plate with the gnocchi and serve.

FLOUNDER fillet rolls
in Shrimp Sauce

 A little more effort   for 4 people   40 minutes

Preparation:

1. Preheat the oven to 350°F (180°C).

2. Peel the onion and garlic, chop fine, and caramelize in hot butter. Sift the flour over them and brown. Pour the broth and wine over them.

3. Wash the parsley, shake dry, chop small, and stir into the sauce. Save 1 tablespoon parsley for garnish. Season the sauce with the lemon juice and red pepper. Mix in the cream and shrimp.

4. Wash the flounder fillets under cold running water, pat dry with paper towels, and halve lengthwise. Season with salt and pepper, roll up, and hold with toothpicks.

5. Put the fillet rolls in a greased baking pan, pour the hot sauce over them, and bake for 20 minutes in the oven.

6. Cook the rice mixture covered in 1²/₃ cups (400ml) of boiling salt water at low heat for 20 minutes, until the rice has absorbed the liquid.

7. Clean the sweet peas and boil 2-3 minutes in salt water until ready to eat.

8. Plate the rice and peas with the fish rolls and sauce. Serve garnished with red pepper and the remaining parsley.

Ingredients:

1 onion and 1 clove garlic	$^{1}/_{3}$ cup (75ml) sweet cream
2 Tbsp butter	$^{1}/_{8}$ lb (90g) cooked shrimp
1-2 Tbsp flour	4 flounder fillets (~ $^{1}/_{4}$ lb [120g] each)
1 $^{1}/_{2}$ cups (360ml) chicken broth	Grease for the pan
3 $^{1}/_{3}$ Tbsp (50ml) dry white wine	1 $^{1}/_{3}$ cups (200g) wild rice mixture
$^{1}/_{2}$ bunch parsley	200 grams sweet peas
2 Tbsp lemon juice	Salt, pepper, and toothpicks
Ground red pepper	

CHICKEN breast
with Cornflakes and Orange Sauce

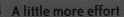 A little more effort — for 4 people — 40 minutes

Ingredients:

4 chicken breasts
($1/3$ - $1/2$ lb [180g] each)

1 egg

1 small package corn flakes

4 Tbsp clarified butter

1 $1/8$ lbs (500g) small potatoes

Juice of 2 oranges

1 $1/3$ Tbsp (2cl) orange liqueur

$3/8$ cup (100ml) sweet cream

1 orange

Salt and pepper

Preparation:

1. Wash the chicken breast under cold running water, pat dry with paper towels, and season with salt and pepper.

2. Beat the egg in a bowl. Crush the corn flakes slightly and put on a plate. Turn the chicken breasts over in the egg, then bread them with the corn flakes.

3. Melt 2 tablespoons of clarified butter in a pan and fry the chicken breasts for 6 minutes on each side.

4. Peel the potatoes, cook 10 minutes in salt water and drain.

5. Mix the meat stock with the orange juice and liqueur and thin with cream. Season to taste with salt and pepper, and place in an oven set to warm along with the chicken breasts.

6. Wash the orange in hot water, pat dry, and use a microplane to make orange zest from the skin.

7. Melt the rest of the clarified butter in a pan and fry the potatoes in it for 10 minutes. Season with salt and pepper.

8. Arrange the chicken breasts, potatoes, and sauce on plates. Serve garnished with orange zest.

> When you cook chicken, make sure that it is cooked all the way through.

PORK TENDERLOIN fillet
and Potato Salad

A little more effort   for 4 people   35 minutes

Preparation:

1. Wash the potatoes and cook 20 minutes with a tea-spoon of salt. Use a pointed paring knife to see if they are done.

2. Peel, quarter, and core the apples, and cut into small cubes. Wash the fillet in cold water and pat dry with paper towels.

3. Heat the olive oil in a pan, sear the whole fillet, and add the peppercorns to the hot pan. Cut the fillet into slices about $^3/_4$ inch (2 cm) thick and brown them again on both sides. Season with salt, pepper, and paprika powder and keep warm in the pan. Make sure the fillet continues to cook in the hot pan.

4. For the marinade, mix the vinegar, lemon juice, soy sauce, mustard, and oil. Season with salt and pepper.

5. Peel the warm potatoes and cut them into slices. Bring the beef bouillon briefly to a boil and immediately pour it over the potato slices and mix well. Let it set until the liquid is absorbed, stirring carefully.

6. Pour the marinade and apple pieces over the potato slices and mix them. Cut the fillet slices into small pieces and add to the potato salad along with the peppercorns. Stir with a large spoon.

7. Cut the cress from the bed. Put the potato salad in a bowl, strew the cress over it, and serve at once.

Ingredients:

1 ⅓ lbs (600g) firm, cooking potatoes	**For the marinade:**
1 pork tenderloin fillet (~1 ⅓ lbs [600g])	2 Tbsp vinegar
¼ cup (30g) green peppercorns	1 Tbsp lemon juice
2 Tbsp oil	1 tsp soy sauce
1 apple	1 tsp mustard
Salt, pepper, and paprika powder	2 Tbsp oil
⅔ cup (150ml) beef bouillon	Salt and pepper
1 cup watercress	

> Ground cherries give this dish a fruity taste. They can be used as a garnish or mixed into the potato salad.

FRUIT dumplings
with Apple-Vanilla Sauce

 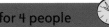

A little more effort   for 4 people   40 minutes

Preparation:

1. Heat the milk with the butter. Add the vanilla extract, $^1/_8$ cup (30g) sugar, and the grits and let it cook for a minute, stirring constantly. Let it cool and mix the eggs in.

2. Peel the apple, remove the core, and dice small. Stir with the remaining sugar and the cinnamon, and heat for 2 minutes. Mix in the peanut brittle and let it cool.

3. Divide the dough into 8 pieces, make a ball of each and press flat. Put a teaspoon of the apple mixture on it and form a dumpling.

4. Let the dumplings cook in water over low heat until they float. Take them out with a slotted spoon and let them drip dry.

5. Mix the vanilla sauce powder with 4 tablespoons of sugar and stir it into some cider with the apple wine. Boil the rest of the cider with the wine, mix in the vanilla sauce, stirring constantly, and let it boil. Refine it with the cream and some cinnamon.

6. Heat the butter with the rest of the sugar. Add the breadcrumbs and roll the dumplings in the mixture. Put the dumplings on plates with the apple-vanilla sauce and garnish with mint leaves.

Ingredients:

For the dumplings:

1 1/2 cups (375ml) milk
3/4 Tbsp (10g) butter
1-2 drops vanilla extract
1/4 cup (40g) sugar
1 1/4 cups flour (125g)
Soft wheat grits
2 eggs
1 apple
2 knife points cinnamon
2 tsp peanut brittle

For the sauce:

2 7/8 oz (2, 40-g packages) vanilla sauce powder
5 Tbsp sugar
3/4 cup (170ml) apple cider
3/4 cup (170ml) apple wine
3/8 cup (100ml) sweet cream
2 Tbsp (30g) butter
1/4 cup (30g) breadcrumbs
Cinnamon

For the garnish:

Fresh mint leaves

COOKING (Etiquette) school

So the evening will be a complete success...

Clinking Glasses

Here's how to do it tastefully: First, lift the glass, then make eye contact with her, wish her good health, drink, make eye contact again, and put the glass down. Normally people do it only with alcoholic drinks. This is no longer the case today. After all, one doesn't want to force a teetotaler to drink.

Utensils

Don't fear a table setting with copious utensils! Simply work from the outside in with each course of the meal.

Forks and Spoons

Your mother probably told you this ad nauseam, but we'll tell you again anyway: always bring your fork or spoon to your mouth and not the other way around.

Glasses

Always pick up wine and champagne glasses by the stem. Thus you avoid warming chilled beverages too quickly with your body heat, which makes them taste dull. This also keeps greasy fingerprints off the glass, which makes for a nicer sound when clinked during a toast.

Posture

Naturally, you should not slump at the table, but sit in an upright and relaxed position. Never support yourself on your elbows. And never place any part of your arm above the wrists on the table.

Coughing and Sneezing

Always hold a hand or napkin in front of your face when you cannot avoid coughing or sneezing at the table. When sneezing, you should always turn quickly away from the table if possible.

Sitting Down

According to the old school, you always adjust the lady's chair before you sit down. Such polite gestures still make a good impression today.

Smoking

Only smoke when the last course is finished, not between the courses of a menu. But even then, you should always seek approval from your companion before lighting up.

Napkins

Don't just stick the napkin into your shirt collar. When you begin to eat, place it on your lap, folded into a square. After a meal the napkin does not belong on top of any remaining food on the plate, but loosely folded to the left of the plate so no stains are showing.

Drinking

If you would like to sip your drink during the meal, wipe your mouth with your napkin first. By doing this you avoid getting unappetizing food and fat smears on the glass.

Just don't do it...

→ Slurping, lip-smacking, sighing, or letting out an audible "Ah!" after taking a sip of your drink are just not funny. But surely you know that already.

→ Don't blow your nose with your napkin. That's what handkerchiefs are for. It is best to turn away from the table when you blow your nose—it is not exactly an appetizing sight.

→ Don't cool the soup by blowing audibly—just wait a minute or two.

→ Don't shovel your food in as though you haven't eaten for days. Eat slowly and properly, not like a half-starved carnivore.

→ Don't suck an entire spaghetti noodle into your mouth or cut it with your knife. Wrap it around your fork, perhaps guiding it with your spoon.

→ And now a old well-known rule that still holds: Never talk with your mouth full. You should spare your companions that not-so-pleasant sight—not to mention it presents a choking hazard. Finish chewing, swallow, then talk!

→ Don't pick bits of food out of your teeth at the table, not even behind your hand or napkin. Save that for the rest room.

The Connoisseur Chooses...

Aperitif:	Prosecco, Campari, martini, kir, port, Manhattan, sherry, etc.
First and main course:	White wine for white meats (poultry, pork, and fish), red wine for red meats (beef and game). A simple ground rule that is easy to remember: the lighter the meat, the lighter the wine!
Sweet desserts:	Lively wine or sparkling wine
Cheese plate	Red wine
Digestive:	Dessert wine (Muscat, Sauternes), brandy (cognac, Armagnac, grappa), fruit brandies (Calvados, Mirabelle), and liqueurs (ouzo, amaretto, limoncello)

So as not to dull the taste buds, one usually drinks light wines before heavy ones, dry before lively, newer vintages before older, and white before red.

BEEF goulash

 The whole enchilada   for 6-8 people   50 minutes prep + 3 hours cooking

Preparation:

1. Preheat the oven to 250°F (120°C).

2. Cut tendons and fat off the beef, wash under cold running water, and let dry.

3. Mix the goulash spices well in a bowl: the strong red paprika, flour, salt, and pepper.

4. Peel and quarter the onions. Peel the garlic and potatoes. Wash the chives, shake dry, and cut fine. Keep a few chives for the garnish.

5. Clean the mushrooms with a mushroom or kitchen brush. Don't wash them in water, they will absorb the water and lose their flavor! Very stubborn dirt can be cut out with a paring knife. Cut off the stem. Use only undamaged mushrooms.

6. Heat 4 tablespoons of oil and brown the meat thoroughly. Take the meat out and put it aside.

7. Sauté the onions and mushrooms in the frying fat and add pressed garlic. Stir in the tomato paste and warm briefly. Add the meat stock and the potatoes to the sauce and stir it all well.

8. Heat the beef briefly in the sauce and then pour the entire stew into a tempered glass baking dish. Bake covered in the oven for about 3 hours. Plate the goulash and serve garnished with chives.

Ingredients:

3 ⅓ lbs (1 ½ kg) cubed beef	½ bunch chives
1 tsp strong red paprika	1 ⅛ lbs (500g) champignon mushrooms
1 Tbsp flour	8 Tbsp oil
2 ¼ lbs (1kg) onions	1 Tbsp tomato paste
1 clove garlic	3 ⅓ cups (800ml) meat stock
¾ lb (350g) potatoes	Salt and pepper

BEEF stroganoff

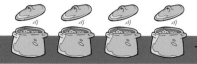

The whole enchilada for 4 people 40 minutes

Preparation:

1. Wash the meat in cold water, pat dry, and cut into ³/₄-inch (2cm) cubes. Peel and dice the onions. Wash the parsley and chives and shake dry. Save a few sprigs of chives for the garnish. Wash, dry, and quarter the tomatoes.

2. Clean the mushrooms with a mushroom or kitchen brush. Don't wash them in water, they will absorb the water and lose their flavor! Very stubborn dirt can be cut out with a paring knife. Cut off the stem. Use only undamaged mushrooms. Cut them into thick slices and sauté in 2 tablespoons of liquid margarine.

3. Melt the clarified butter in a frying pan and brown the meat. Take it out and keep it warm.

4. Cook the noodles according to the package. Drain and let drip dry before they get too soft.

5. Sauté the diced onions in frying fat and add the instant roasting sauce powder. Cool with 4 cups (1l) of water. Mix the flour in 1 cup (¹/₄ l) cold water, add the mixture to the sauce and bring to a boil. Puree with a hand mixer and refine with the cooking cream. Season with salt and pepper.

6. Add the beef fillet and mushrooms to the sauce and briefly bring to a boil.

7. Garnish the beef Stroganoff with parsley, chives, and tomato quarters and serve with the noodles.

Ingredients:

1 ³/₄ lbs (800g) beef fillet	3 cups (200g) champignon mushrooms sliced	Salt and pepper
¹/₃ cup (70g) clarified butter	2 Tbsp liquid margarine	
6 onions (~1 ¹/₈ lbs [500g])	1 cup (40g) parsley	**As side dish:**
2 Tbsp instant roasting sauce	¹/₂ bunch chives	1, 16-oz bag of egg noodles
¹/₂ cup (¹/₈ l) cooking cream	2 tomatoes	(500g)
1 Tbsp flour		

SAVOY CABBAGE wrap

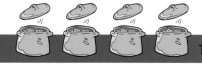 The whole enchilada for 4 people ⏱ 50 minutes

Ingredients:

1 head Savoy cabbage
3 $^1/_3$ Tbsp (50ml) vinegar
2 $^1/_4$ lbs (1kg) ground beef
2 onions
3-5 Tbsp oil
1 Tbsp Worcestershire sauce
1 Tbsp salt
1 Tbsp pepper and nutmeg
2 eggs
2 stale rolls
$^1/_3$ lb (200g) bacon (cubed)
1 cup ($^1/_4$ l) broth
1-2 tsp sauce thickener (arrowroot or potato starch)
Kitchen string

Preparation:

1. Clean the cabbage and cut out the stem in a wedge shape. Boil 5 $^1/_3$ qt (5l) of salt water with the vinegar. Cook the cabbage until the outer leaves come loose easily. Take out of the water, remove the 6 outermost leaves, and lay them on paper towels. Cut the thickest ribs of the leaves flat by holding the knife parallel to the cutting board.

2. Soften the rolls in water. Peel the onions and dice small.

3. Mix the ground beef with the squeezed rolls, onions, eggs, Worcestershire sauce, salt, pepper, and nutmeg. Divide the mixture evenly and place on the cabbage leaves. Roll them up and tie them together with kitchen string.

4. Heat the oil in a frying pan. Brown the cabbage wraps on all sides. Add the bacon and brown it. Pour on the broth. Let the wraps simmer for about 50 minutes on low heat.

5. Thicken the broth with the sauce thickener and season as you wish. Potatoes are a tasty side dish for these wraps.

> Cut the rest of the Savoy cabbage into thin strips. Sauté a finely diced onion in some oil, add the Savoy, and cook briefly while stirring. Pour on some broth and cook for 20 minutes. If necessary, thicken with a sauce thickener. Season to taste with salt, pepper, and nutmeg.

ROAST beef
with Swabian-style* Onions

 The whole enchilada   for 4 people   25 minutes

Ingredients:

4 rump steaks
(~1/3 lb [150g] each)
4 Tbsp sunflower oil
14 oz (400g) noodles
4 onions
Fresh parsley
Salt and pepper

Preparation:

1. Wash the rump steaks under cold running water, pat dry with paper towels, pound the meat a few times to square the edges. Coat with some oil and let the meat set for a few minutes.

2. Cook the noodles as per the package instructions. Drain them and let them drip dry before they get too soft.

3. Heat the rest of the oil in a pan and brown the rump steaks thoroughly on all sides. Cook for another 3-4 minutes on each side. Take the steaks out of the pan, add salt and pepper, and keep warm.

4. Peel the onions, cut into rings, and fry them well in the remaining roasting fat.

5. Arrange the steaks on plates with the onion rings and noodles. Garnish with parsley. White cabbage salad is a refreshing side dish.

* Swabia is a region in southwestern Germany that occupies much of the state of Baden-Württemberg. The region has its own German dialect and cuisine.

STEAK with beans
Wrapped in Bacon

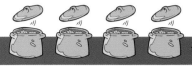

 The whole enchilada — for 4 people — 40 minutes

Preparation:

1. Wash and clean the beans. Cook 4 minutes in boiling salt water without a lid. Then chill in an ice water bath to stop the cooking process and keep the beans' green color.

2. Wrap every six beans with a bacon strip. The thinner the bacon, the more easily it can be wrapped around the beans. Melt the clarified butter in a pan and brown the bean bundles on all sides.

3. Wash the steaks in cold water and pat dry. Heat the clarified butter in the pan and brown the steaks well for 8-10 minutes.

4. Regularly test the steaks with a fork to see when they are finished. Before serving, season to taste with salt and pepper.

   * Choosing the right moment takes experience. If it feels firm, take it out of the pan quickly—otherwise it's shoe leather.

5. Cook the noodles according to the package. Drain and let drip dry before they get too soft.

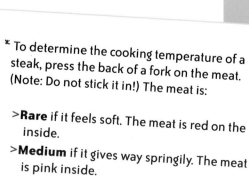

* To determine the cooking temperature of a steak, press the back of a fork on the meat. (Note: Do not stick it in!) The meat is:

>**Rare** if it feels soft. The meat is red on the inside.

>**Medium** if it gives way springily. The meat is pink inside.

>**Well done** if it feels firm. The meat is now cooked evenly throughout.

Ingredients:

For the steaks:	For the beans:	Side dish:
4 beef steaks	1 $\frac{1}{8}$ lbs (500g) green beans	1, 16-oz bag of egg noodles
(~ $\frac{1}{2}$ lb each [250g])	$\frac{1}{2}$ lb (200g) sliced bacon	(500g)
$\frac{1}{4}$ cup (50g) clarified butter	1 Tbsp clarified butter	
Salt and pepper		

ROAST beef
with Cheese-Polenta Crust

Preparation:

1. Preheat the oven to 400°F (200°C).

2. Wash the beef under cold running water and pat dry with paper towels.

3. Crush the Brazilian pepper berries crudely, mix with the orange juice and salt, and rub on the roast beef. Heat the oil in a frying pan and sear the beef on all sides.

4. Peel and crush the garlic and sauté it in some melted butter. Add the milk and the rest of the butter and bring to a boil. Sprinkle in the polenta and stir until the mixture loosens from the bottom. Let it cool somewhat.

5. Grate the cheese. Separate the egg and mix the yolk into the polenta. Beat the egg white stiff and fold into the polenta with the cheese.

6. Wash the herbs, shake dry, and chop small. Season the polenta with salt, pepper, and herbs. Spread the polenta on the beef and roast in the oven for 5 minutes per centimeter of the roast's height, including the crust.

7. Peel the onion, dice, and simmer in the meat stock. Add the Brazilian peppercorns and tomato paste. Bring to a boil and season with salt and pepper. Puree the sauce. Add a few Brazilian pepper berries for decoration.

8. Wash the field green salad thoroughly and let it drip dry in a colander. Wash, clean, and cut the strawberries into pieces. Make a dressing of salt, pepper, white wine vinegar, and walnut oil. Pour it on the salad.

9. Carve the roast beef into thick slices and plate with the sauce and field salad. Serve garnished with the strawberries.

Ingredients:

For the roast beef:	For the crust:	For the sauce:	For the field green salad:
1 ³/₄ lbs (800g) beef roast	1 clove garlic	1 onion	1, 8-oz bag of prepared field greens salad mix
1 tsp Brazilian pepper berries	¹/₄ cup (50g) butter	2 Tbsp Brazilian pepper berries	12 strawberries
Juice of ¹/₂ an orange	⁷/₈ cup (200ml) milk	1 Tbsp tomato paste	4 Tbsp white wine vinegar
1 tsp salt	¹/₄ cup (60g) corn polenta	1 cup (250ml) broth	4 Tbsp walnut oil
2 Tbsp cooking oil	1 ¹/₃ cups (150g) swiss cheese (shredded)	1 ²/₃ cups (400ml) sweet cream	Salt and pepper
	1 egg	Salt and pepper	
	Several marjoram and oregano leaves		
	Salt and freshly ground pepper		

Festive
SAUERbraten

The whole enchilada   for 4 people   90-105 minutes + 4-5 days to marinate

Preparation:

1. Peel the shallots and carrot and cube them. Cook them with the vinegar, red wine, bay leaf, cloves, and peppercorns.

2. Wash the beef under cold running water, pat dry with paper towels, and put in the above mixture for 4-5 days

3. Take the meat out of the marinade, pat dry, sprinkle with salt and the spice mix, and brown in the heated oil.

4. Pour on the marinade and the broth, bring to a boil, and stew covered for 60-80 minutes. Take the meat out and keep it warm.

5. Pour the sauce into a pot through a sieve. Add the halved baking plums and the plum puree. Season with salt and pepper and thicken with a dark sauce thickener.

6. Wash the potatoes for the dumplings and cook for 20 minutes in salt water until done. Drain the potatoes, let them cool somewhat, peel, then mash. Melt the butter and add to the potatoes along with the egg. Gradually work the starch in, then season with salt, pepper, and nutmeg. Make 12 dumplings from the dough and cook them for 10 minutes in very hot salt water.

7. Heat the red cabbage according to the package directions. Carve the roast into slices and arrange on the plates along with the red cabbage, dumplings, and sauce. Garnish with parsley.

Ingredients:

For the marinade:	For the roast:	For the dumplings:
2 shallots	1 ³/₄ lbs (800g) beef roast	⁷/₈ lb (400g) potatoes
1 carrot	1 tsp sea salt	1 Tbsp butter
¹/₂ cup (120ml) Balsamic vinegar	1 ¹/₂ tsp pumpkin pie, apple pie,	1 egg
1 ²/₃ cups (400ml) red wine	or Chinese five-spice mix	4 Tbsp starch
1 bay leaf	(or mix them 1:1:1)	Salt and pepper
3 cloves	2 Tbsp cooking oil	Ground nutmeg
¹/₂ tsp peppercorns	⁷/₈ cup (200ml) broth	
	12 soft baking plums	Also:
	2 Tbsp plum puree	1 jar red cabbage (24 oz [720 ml])
	Dark sauce thickener	Fresh parsley for garnish
	Salt and freshly ground pepper	

> A ready-made herb mixture can also be used for the meat. Or you can buy the sauerbraten already flavored and refine the sauce, for example, with apple pie, pumpkin pie, or Chinese five-spice mixture.

ONION soup

The whole enchilada for 4 people | 30 minutes

Ingredients:

6 onions
$1/3$ cup (70g) clarified butter
4 cups (1l) meat or vegetable broth
Salt and pepper
Grated nutmeg
1 bowl watercress
1 cup (120g) grated cheese
4 slices toasting bread

Preparation:

1. Peel the onions and cut into rings.

2. Melt the clarified butter in a large pot and sauté the onions in it. Season with pepper.

3. Pour in the meat or vegetable broth and let it cook briefly. Season with salt, pepper, and nutmeg.

4. Put the onion soup into tempered bowls and lay a piece of toasting bread on top of each, then sprinkle with cheese.

5. Bake under the broiler for 5-10 minutes at 425°F (220°C), until the cheese is a golden brown color. Add the watercress as a garnish.

Cutting onions is not for softies ... With these tips you can do the job without tears:

> Always use a sharp knife, so the onion fibers are crushed less and thus less juice comes out.

> Don't hold your head directly over the cutting board, since the vapors rise.

> Cut the onions under a smoke hood that's on. The gases will be sucked away.

> Spare your mouth—don't breathe the onion in with your mouth open.

> Put a burning candle near the cutting board.

> If nothing else helps, wear goggles and a respirator mask.

Roasted
SALMON steaks
with Dumplings and Spinach

The whole enchilada   for 4 people   25 minutes

Preparation:

1. Preheat the oven to 425°F (220°C).

2. Wash the salmon steaks under cold running water and pat dry with paper towels. Season with lemon pepper and put a patty of herbal butter on top each one. Put the salmon in a baking pan and bake in the oven for 10-15 minutes.

3. Prepare the mini-dumplings according to the instructions on the package.

4. Take the spinach leaves off the stems and wash them. Heat ²/₃ cup (150ml) water in a large pot with a pinch of salt. Add the spinach, gather it with a sieve, then let it drip dry.

5. Peel the pearl onions and garlic and dice small. Melt the clarified butter in a pot and sauté the garlic and onions in it. Add the spinach and season with salt, pepper, and nutmeg.

6. Arrange the salmon steaks on the plates with the mini-dumplings and spinach. Sprinkle the cheese over them and serve garnished with tarragon.

Ingredients:

4 salmon steaks	For the spinach:
4 patties herb butter	2, 10-oz packages of fresh leaf spinach (600g)
14 oz (400 g) mini-dumpling mix	4 pearl onions
¹/₂ cup (50g) grated cheese	2 cloves garlic
Lemon pepper	2 Tbsp clarified butter
Fresh tarragon	Ground nutmeg

Grilled
SALMON cakes

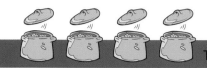 The whole enchilada for 4 people · 30 minutes prep + 2 hour marinade

Ingredients:

1 ⅛ lbs (500g) sea salmon fillet
2 slices toast
3 ⅓ Tbsp (50ml) sweet cream
2 pearl onions
1 small red pepper
1 egg
Salt and freshly ground pepper

For the potato salad:
1 ⅛ lbs (500g) firm cooking potatoes
2 apples
1 bunch chives
1 tsp mustard
5 Tbsp sunflower oil
2-3 Tbsp white balsamic vinegar
Salt and freshly ground pepper
Sugar

Preparation:

1. Wash the potatoes for the potato salad and cook 20 minutes in salt water. Don't let them get too soft, or they'll fall apart. Drain them, peel them while still warm, and cut into slices.

2. Wash the apples, quarter, core, and cut the quarters into slices. Wash the chives, shake dry, and cut into small pieces. Save a few chive stems for garnish.

3. Mix the mustard with the oil and vinegar and season with salt, pepper, and sugar. Mix with the salad ingredients and let sit for 2 hours if possible.

4. Wash the salmon fillets under cold running water, pat dry with paper towels, and cube. Remove the crust from the toast and cube it.

5. Mix the fish and toast, pour cream over them and puree in the mixer.

6. Wash and dry the pearl onions and cut them into fine rings. Halve the red pepper, remove the membrane and seeds, wash, and dice very small. Knead both equally into the fish with the egg and season with salt and pepper.

7. With slightly dampened hands, make eight cakes of the fish mixture and press them flat. Pan fry for 4 minutes on each side in a frying pan or on oiled aluminum foil on the grill.

8. Season the salad again and arrange on plates with the fish cakes. Serve garnished with the remaining chives.

CHOCOLATE mouse

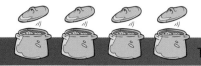

The whole enchilada for 6 people 20 minutes prep + chilling overnight

Preparation:

1. Chop the topping and the chocolate small and let them melt in a hot water bath, stirring them.

2. Separate the eggs and beat the egg white with the sugar. Mix the yolks with the vanilla sugar until frothy and beat the cream stiff.

3. Mix the melted, lukewarm chocolate into the egg yolk-vanilla sugar mixture. Carefully stir in the cream and then immediately fold in the egg whites.

4. Pour the chocolate into a flat form and refrigerate for at least 3 hours. It's best to leave it overnight.

5. Wash, clean, peel, and cut the strawberries and mangos into slices for a garnish. Arrange the slices in fans.

6. Cut pieces out of the solidified mousse with a knife dipped into hot water. Make sure to cut the pieces large enough so they retain a nice shape.

7. Place one or two pieces of mousse on each plate, garnish with the fruit fans and fresh lemon balm, and grate chocolate directly over the plates with a scraper or paring knife.

Ingredients:

For the mousse:	For the garnish:
5 ⅓ oz (150g) semi-bitter chocolate	6 strawberries
1 ¾ oz (50g) chocolate with coffee flavor	2 mangos
5 fresh eggs	Fresh lemon balm
½ cup (100g) sugar	Milk chocolate for grated topping
3 packages vanilla sugar	
½ cup (⅛ l) sweet cream	

> Absolutely fresh and healthy eggs are the alpha and omega here! When you make chocolate mousse, the eggs may not be heated high enough to kill off bacteria. The danger of salmonella should not be underrated!

Index

Cooking Together: Having Fun with Two or More Cooks in the Kitchen,
978-0-7643-3647-8, $19.99
Cooking with Mustard: Empowering your Palate,
978-0-7643-3643-0, $19.99

Today I Cook: A Man's Guide to the Kitchen,
978-0-7643-3644-7, $19.99
Creative Ideas for Garnishing & Decorating,
978-0-7643-3645-4, $19.99
Asparagus & Strawberries,
978-0-7643-3648-5, $19.99

Originally published as *Heute koche ich!* by Edition XXL

Translated from the German by Dr. Edward Force
Concept and Project Leader: Sonja Sammueller
Layout, Typsetting, and Cover: Sammueller Kreativ GMBH

The contents of this book were checked carefully by the author and publisher, who will accept no liability for personal or physical property damage.

Type set in Bailey Sans ITC/JensHand/Palatino
ISBN: 978-0-7643-3644-7
Printed in China

Schiffer Books are available at special discounts for bulk purchases for sales promotions or premiums. Special editions, including personalized covers, corporate imprints, and excerpts can be created in large quantities for special needs. For more information contact the publisher:

Published by Schiffer Publishing Ltd.
4880 Lower Valley Road
Atglen, PA 19310
Phone: (610) 593-1777; Fax: (610) 593-2002
E-mail: Info@schifferbooks.com

For the largest selection of fine reference books on this and related subjects, please visit our web site atWe are always looking for people to write books on new and related subjects. If you have an idea for a book please contact us at the above address.

This book may be purchased from the publisher. Include $5.00 for shipping. Please try your bookstore first. You may write for a free catalog.

In Europe, Schiffer books are distributed by
Bushwood Books
6 Marksbury Ave.
Kew Gardens
Surrey TW9 4JF England
Phone: 44 (0) 20 8392 8585; Fax: 44 (0) 20 8392 9876
E-mail: info@bushwoodbooks.co.uk
Website: www.bushwoodbooks.co.uk

Photo Credits

We thank the following firms for their friendly assistance:
Fisch-Informationszentrum (FIZ), Hamburg: 14, 34, 49, 76-77
State Organization of the Bavarian Milk Industry: 20, 39
Molkerei Weihenstephan: 15
MPR Dr. Muth Public Relations, Hamburg: USA Rice Federation: 3, 50-51
Peter Koelln, Elmshorn: 10-11
Supress Press Service, Duesseldorf: 52-53
The Food Professionals Koehnen, Sprockhoevel: Fuchs: 35, 36-37; Grafschafter: 41;
    Goldpuder: 40, 56-57; Henglein: 74-75; Kuehne: 3, 70-71; Leerdammer: 68-69;
    Ostmann: 21; Squpiquet: 38, 48; Wirths PR, Fischach; www.1000rezepte.de: 29, 65;
    Zottarella: 12-13
All other photos: Sammueller Kreativ GmbH